ANIMALS!

Illustrated by the Hildebrandts

Platt & Munk, Publishers/New York
A Division of Grosset & Dunlap

The Anteater

The anteater is one of the few toothless land animals, but that doesn't discourage it from eating. It claws through the rock-hard termite and ant mounds of British Honduras and reaches down as far as 20 inches with its long tongue to eat eggs and insects.

The Peacock

The peacock lives in the forests of India and Ceylon. Famous for the beauty of its tail feathers, the peacock enjoys strutting about with its tail fully fanned. The female of the species, the peahen, is less brightly colored.

The Wolverine

The wolverine is a weak-sighted animal that lives in the wilds of North America. The wolverine is something of a bandit. It waits until a family leaves the house. Then it steals in and eats all the food it can find. The wolverine also steals bait from hunters' traps.

The Fox

The fox is a member of the dog family, but unlike most dogs, its strongest sense is sight. Like most sharp-eyed animals, it sleeps days and hunts nights. The fox runs fast, using its tail as a rudder. It sleeps snugly, using its tail as a pillow.

The Hippopotamus

The hippopotamus wades in water over its head to graze on the grass that grows on the river bottom. When it comes up for air, only its eyes and nose show above the water. The baby hippo is born under water and rides on its mother's back until it has learned to swim.

The Dolphin

The dolphin is one of the most intelligent animals in the world. Through a blowhole in its forehead, it "speaks" a language consisting of whistles, grunts, barks, and squeaks. The dolphin is a mammal, not a fish, and has no gills for underwater breathing. Every few minutes, it must surface for oxygen.

The Black-necked Swan

The black-necked swan lives high in the Andes mountains in South America. Before her young can fly by themselves, mother swan flies with her babies on her back. While she swims, they nap between her wings, or swim nearby.

The Three-toed Sloth

The three-toed sloth is native to the forests of Honduras and northern Argentina. As its name suggests, the sloth is slow-moving. It spends most of its life hanging by its claws from branches, feeding on the thick juicy leaves of the cecropia tree.

The Leopard

The black and brown spots that cover the leopard's yellow coat help it to blend into the shadows of leafy trees. It is high in the trees that the leopard spends much of its life. The leopard leaps to attack its prey from the trees, eats in the trees, and even sleeps in the trees.

The Opossum

The opossum is born only partly developed and spends the first month of its life attached to its mother in a pouch on her stomach. The expression "to play possum" comes from the Virginia opossum's habit of pretending to be dead when in danger.

The Sea Otter

The sea otter is one of the few animals that eats with a tool. It dives for clams on the ocean floor. It selects a clam and a rock and carries both to the surface. Floating on its back, it puts the rock on its chest and bangs the shell against the rock to crack it.

The Gorilla

Largest of the great apes, the lowland gorilla lives in the forests of Central Africa. The gorilla is thought to be a fierce beast, but it is really harmless. When strangers near its family band, a father gorilla will rush up to them, pounding its chest and bellowing. But it's all a show. Gorillas almost never attack.

The Spider Monkey

The spider monkey is so called because of its slender torso and long arms and tail. It uses its tail like a fifth arm, wrapping it around branches and swinging from tree to tree in the jungles of Mexico, Bolivia, and southern Brazil.

The Zebra

Everybody knows the zebra by its black and white stripes, but there are three different kinds of zebra, each with slightly different striping, all found only on the continent of Africa. The largest, pictured below, is Grevy's zebra, which weighs as much as 800 pounds. Like a horse, the zebra eats grass and travels in a herd.

The Giraffe

Growing as tall as 18 feet, the giraffe is the world's tallest animal. With its long neck, it can reach high into the trees and feed on the topmost leaves.

The Elephant

The elephant is the largest living land animal. The African bush elephant, pictured below, can weigh as much as 13,000 pounds. The elephant's trunk is five or six feet long. The elephant uses its trunk as a trumpet to sound a warning, as a hose to drink from and bathe with, and as a hand to pick up objects from the ground and pick fruits from the trees.

The Rhinoceros

The rhinoceros lives in Asia and Africa. It has extremely poor eyesight. Possibly because of its poor eyesight, the rhinoceros is an unpredictable creature, reacting to the scent of nearby humans sometimes by charging away from them, sometimes toward them, at the speed of 35 miles per hour.

The Wolf

A male and female wolf stay together as a couple for life. Each spring, they dig a den in which to raise their young cubs. The rest of the year, they travel in packs and hunt.

The Raccoon

The raccoon is known for its black mask and ringed tail, and for the neatness of its eating habits. The raccoon washes its food before eating it. All summer long, the raccoon hunts for small animals and makes a nuisance of itself turning over garbage cans and stealing chickens. All winter long, it sleeps, curled in the stump of a hollow tree.

The Fox Squirrel

The fox squirrel of North America is a master engineer. Every winter, it builds an insulated nest in which to hibernate. From twigs and damp leaves, it weaves a globe-shaped nest with two walls. All winter the fox squirrel sleeps, and its own body heat, trapped within the two-walled nest, keeps it warm and snug.